COCKTAILS

Publications International, Ltd.

All recipes and photographs on pages 19, 20, 23, 24, 27, 28, 31, 32, 36, 39, 40, 43, 44, 47, 51, 56, 59, 63, 67, 68, 71, 74, 77, 78, 82, 89, 92, 94, 97, 99, 100, 103, 111, 116, 132, 135, 138, 143, 148, 151, 152, 155, 156, 159, 162, 166, 173, 178, 181, 182, 185 and 186 copyright © Publications International, Ltd.

Photographs on front cover and pages 1, 4, 5, 6, 7, 8, 10, 13, 16, 48, 52, 60, 64, 81, 85, 86, 104, 108, 112, 115, 119, 120, 123, 124, 128, 131, 136, 140, 144, 161, 169, 170 and 174 copyright © Shutterstock.com.

Pictured on the back cover *(clockwise from top left):* Tuxedo Cocktail *(page 42),* Moscow Mule *(page 122),* Cranberry Caipirinha *(page 25),* West Side *(page 117)* and Bloody Mary *(page 125).*

ISBN: 978-1-68022-540-2

Library of Congress Control Number: 2016939496

Manufactured in China.

8 7 6 5 4 3 2 1

Publications International, Ltd.

CONTENTS

COCKTAIL BASICS

*Timeless **and** trendy? Yes! The wonderful world of cocktails combines the stylish classics that have been around for decades with fresh new twists that keep things exciting. You don't need to immerse yourself in cocktail culture to enjoy it, but some basic bar knowledge will make creating great cocktails easy—and fun!*

Start with the fundamentals, such as getting the right tools and stocking the bar. The following pages will show you what you'll need to prepare the recipes in this book.

BAR TOOLS

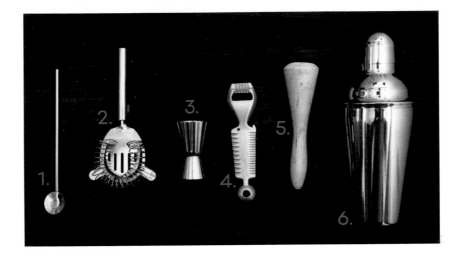

BAR SPOON: A long-handled metal spoon to stir drinks in a mixing glass or other tall glass (1).

BLENDER: A necessary tool for making ice cream drinks and slushy drinks like frozen daiquiris or smoothies. Also useful for crushing ice.

CHANNEL KNIFE: An inexpensive tool with a metal tooth for peeling long thin twists from citrus fruit for garnishing (4).

CITRUS JUICER: Can be anything from a simple wooden reamer or metal press to a fancy electric juicer.

CORKSCREW: A waiter's corkscrew is a popular style which includes a small blade to cut the from wine caps as well as a bottle opener.

JIGGER: A two-sided stainless steel measuring tool, preferably with 1- and 1½-ounce cups (3).

MIXING GLASS: A large glass (at least 16 ounces) used for shaking or stirring drinks with ice to chill them.

MUDDLER: A long sturdy tool—usually made of wood—used to crush ingredients like herbs, fresh fruit and sugar (5).

SHAKER: A standard metal cocktail shaker is the most common style, which includes the container, a lid with a built-in strainer and a cap for the lid (6).

STRAINER: To mix drinks in a mixing glass, a Hawthorne bar strainer—flat with a spring coil around its edge—is necessary to keep the ice and muddled fruit out of your drinks (2).

OTHER TOOLS FROM YOUR KITCHEN THAT ARE ALSO USEFUL AT THE BAR:

- Cutting board
- Measuring spoons
- Paring knife
- Pitcher
- Tongs
- Vegetable peeler

GLASSWARE

Don't worry—you don't need all of these glasses in your home bar! Think about what you like to drink and what you typically serve to guests, then purchase accordingly. (Some of them can do double duty.)

CHAMPAGNE FLUTE
4 to 10 ounces

COCKTAIL (also called a martini glass)
3 to 10 ounces

COLLINS
12 to 14 ounces, taller and narrower than a highball glass, often used for drinks served over ice

COUPE
shallow with a wide mouth

HIGHBALL
10 to 12 ounces, tall and narrow to preserve the fizz in drinks with tonic or soda water

HURRICANE
12 to 16 ounces, shaped like a hurricane lamp and used for hurricanes and other tropical drinks

MARGARITA
12 to 14 ounces, used for margaritas and daiquiris

OLD FASHIONED (also called a rocks glass)
4 to 8 ounces, short and wide-mouthed for spirits served neat or drinks served over ice (double old fashioned glasses hold 12 to 16 ounces)

PILSNER GLASS
tall, thin, flared glass used for beer or oversize drinks

SHOT GLASS
1 to 3 ounces, used for shooters and for measuring

WHITE WINE
6 to 12 ounces

RED WINE
8 to 24 ounces

STOCKING THE BAR

Buy what you like and what you'll use most. The better the ingredients, the better your drinks will be. (But keep in mind that the most expensive ingredients aren't always the best ones.)

SPIRITS	MIXERS
• Brandy	• Citrus juices (fresh lemon, lime and orange)
• Champagne or other sparkling wine	• Club soda
• Gin	• Cola
• Liqueurs (almond, coffee, maraschino and orange flavors are some of the most common)	• Ginger ale
	• Lemon-lime soda
• Rum	• Tomato juice (plain or spicy)
• Tequila	• Tonic water
• Vodka	• Water (plain or sparkling)
• Whiskey (bourbon, Scotch, etc.)	• Whipping cream
• Wine (including fortified wines like port, sherry and vermouth)	

FLAVORINGS	GARNISHES
• Bitters	• Celery
• Grenadine	• Lemons
• Hot pepper sauce	• Limes
• Salt (coarse)	• Maraschino cherries
• Sugar (granulated and superfine or powdered)	• Mint sprigs
• Worcestershire sauce	• Olives
	• Oranges

SEASONAL CELEBRATIONS

While many drinks are year-round classics, cocktails, just like cooking, can change with the seasons.

SPRING: Stir up simple, cool refreshing drinks such as Pimm's Cup (page 45) or Buck's Fizz (page 163).

SUMMER: Try fresh, fruity, thirst-quenching drinks like Blackberry Mule (page 122), Shandy (page 168) or Aperol Spritz (page 158).

FALL: Drinks with intense autumn flavors, colors and spices take center stage, like Stone Fence (page 172), Manzarita (page 96) and Cider Sangria (page 171).

WINTER: Serve fun and festive drinks to toast the holidays, such as a Pomegranate Mimosa (page 149) or Cranberry Caipiriha (page 25). Or warm up your guests with hot drinks like Mulled Wine (page 160) or a Hot Toddy (page 130).

TIPS & TRICKS OF THE TRADE

• Use only fresh fruit juices for the best drinks. If you can't squeeze your own, make sure the juice you purchase from the store is labeled "not from concentrate." And always wash your citrus fruits before juicing them or making garnishes.

• Chilled glasses keep your cocktails cool much longer than room-temperature glasses. To chill glasses, put them in the freezer for 30 minutes or in the refrigerator for several hours before preparing your drinks. Or you can fill a glass with crushed ice and let it stand while you mix the drink. Dump out the ice when you're ready to pour the drink.

• Make sure your mixers are cold! When you've gone to the trouble of chilling your glasses, you don't want to warm up your cocktails with room temperature mixers.

• Many recipes call for filling a cocktail shaker with ice—the ice should fill the shaker half to two-thirds full. Usually the ice is added first so it chills the shaker and the ingredients as they are added.

• Pour a cocktail from the shaker or mixing glass immediately after shaking or stirring—letting it stand will dilute the drink.

• Drinks with egg whites, such as Ramos Gin Fizz (page 41), need to be shaken extra vigorously to incorporate the egg white. Use the freshest eggs possible, or you can use pasteurized eggs. (Do not use egg substitutes.)

• When serving hot drinks, make sure the glasses or cups are made of heatproof glass.

CONVERSION CHART

¼ ounce = ½ tablespoon	6 ounces = ¾ cup
½ ounce = 1 tablespoon	8 ounces = 1 cup
¾ ounce = 1½ tablespoons	16 ounces = 2 cups
1 ounce = 2 tablespoons	24 ounces = 3 cups
2 ounces = ¼ cup	32 ounces = 1 quart
4 ounces = ½ cup	

BRANDY

PISCO SOUR

- 2 ounces pisco
- 1 ounce lime juice
- ¼ ounce simple syrup (recipe follows)
- ½ egg white
- 1 dash Angostura bitters

Fill cocktail shaker half full with ice; add pisco, lime juice, simple syrup and egg white. Shake until blended; strain into chilled cocktail glass. Sprinkle foam with bitters.

Simple Syrup: Bring 1 cup water to a boil; stir in 1 cup sugar. Reduce heat to low; stir constantly until sugar is dissolved. Cool to room temperature; store syrup in glass jar in refrigerator.

HOT MULLED CIDER

Makes 16 servings

½ gallon apple cider (nonalcoholic)

½ cup packed brown sugar

½ tablespoon balsamic or cider vinegar

1 teaspoon vanilla

1 cinnamon stick

6 whole cloves

½ cup applejack or bourbon

Combine apple cider, brown sugar, vinegar, vanilla, cinnamon and cloves in large saucepan; bring to a boil over medium-high heat. Reduce heat to low; simmer 30 minutes. Remove and discard cinnamon stick and cloves. Stir in applejack. Serve warm.

VIEUX CARRÉ

Makes 1 serving

- ¾ ounce cognac
- ¾ ounce rye whiskey
- ¾ sweet vermouth
- ½ teaspoon Benedictine
- 3 dashes Angostura bitters
- Lemon twist

Fill mixing glass or cocktail shaker with ice; add cognac, whiskey, vermouth, Benedictine and bitters. Stir until blended; strain into ice-filled old fashioned glass or cocktail glass. Garnish with lemon twist.

BRANDY COLLINS

Makes 1 serving

2 ounces brandy

1 ounce lemon juice

1 teaspoon powdered sugar

3 ounces chilled club soda

Orange slice and maraschino cherry

Fill cocktail shaker half full with ice; add brandy, lemon juice and powdered sugar. Shake until blended; strain into ice-filled Collins glass. Add club soda; stir until blended. Garnish with orange slice and maraschino cherry.

CRANBERRY CAIPIRINHA

2 lime wedges

1 orange wedge

12 fresh cranberries

2 tablespoons packed brown sugar

2 ounces cachaça

1 ounce cranberry juice

Lime twist or slice

Muddle lime wedges, orange wedge, cranberries and brown sugar in mixing glass or cocktail shaker. Add cachaça and cranberry juice; shake until blended. Strain into ice-filled old fashioned glass; garnish with lime twist.

EGGNOG

Makes 1 serving

1½ ounces brandy

¼ to ½ cup milk

2 teaspoons simple syrup (recipe follows)

1 pasteurized egg

¼ teaspoon vanilla (optional)

Ground nutmeg

Fill cocktail shaker half full with ice; add brandy, milk, simple syrup, egg and vanilla, if desired. Shake until blended; strain into mug, highball glass or wine glass. Sprinkle with nutmeg.

Simple Syrup: Bring 1 cup water to a boil; stir in 1 cup sugar. Reduce heat to low; stir constantly until sugar is dissolved. Cool to room temperature; store syrup in glass jar in refrigerator.

Variation: Blend brandy, milk, syrup, egg and vanilla in blender; pour into glass. Sprinkle with nutmeg.

FRENCH CONNECTION

FRENCH CONNECTION

Makes 1 serving

1½ ounces cognac

¾ ounce amaretto

Fill old fashioned glass three-fourths full with ice; add cognac and amaretto. Stir gently until blended.

French Connection No. 2: Substitute orange-flavored liqueur for the amaretto.

STINGER

Makes 1 serving

2 ounces brandy

¾ ounce white crème de menthe

Fill cocktail shaker half full with ice; add brandy and crème de menthe. Shake until blended; strain into chilled cocktail glass.

VICEROY

Makes 1 serving

1½   ounces pisco

1   ounce Lillet Blanc

½   ounce lime juice

½   ounce simple syrup (recipe follows)

1½   ounces tonic water

    Fresh mint sprig

Combine pisco, Lillet Blanc, lime juice and simple syrup in ice-filled highball glass. Top with tonic water; stir gently until blended. Garnish with mint.

Simple Syrup: Bring 1 cup water to a boil; stir in 1 cup sugar. Reduce heat to low; stir constantly until sugar is dissolved. Cool to room temperature; store syrup in glass jar in refrigerator.

JACK ROSE

JACK ROSE

Makes 1 serving

2 ounces applejack

¾ ounce lime juice

¾ ounce grenadine

Lime slice or wedge

Fill cocktail shaker with ice; add applejack, lime juice and grenadine. Shake about 15 seconds or until cold; strain into chilled cocktail glass or coupe. Garnish with lime slice.

SIDECAR

Makes 1 serving

2 ounces brandy or Cognac

2 ounces orange-flavored liqueur

½ ounce lemon juice

Fill cocktail shaker half full with ice; add brandy, liqueur and lemon juice. Shake until blended; strain into chilled cocktail glass.

GIN

GIN
ST. CLEMENT'S

Makes 1 serving

1½ ounces gin

1 ounce lemon juice

1 ounce orange juice

2 ounces tonic water

Orange and/or lemon slices

Fill Collins or highball glass with ice; add gin, lemon juice and orange juice. Top with tonic water; stir until blended. Garnish with orange slice.

MARTINEZ

Makes 1 serving

1½ ounces gin

¾ ounce sweet vermouth

½ ounce maraschino-flavored liqueur

2 dashes orange bitters

Lemon or orange twist

Fill mixing glass with ice; add gin, vermouth, liqueur and bitters. Stir about 20 seconds or until very cold; strain into chilled coupe or cocktail glass. Garnish with lemon twist.

VESPER

Makes 1 serving

3 ounces gin

1 ounce vodka

½ ounce Lillet Blanc

Lemon twist

Fill cocktail shaker with ice; add gin, vodka and Lillet Blanc. Shake until blended; strain into chilled cocktail glass. Garnish with lemon twist.

MARTINEZ

RAMOS GIN FIZZ

Makes 1 serving

2 ounces gin

1 ounce whipping cream

½ ounce lemon juice

½ ounce lime juice

1 teaspoon superfine sugar

2 dashes orange flower water

1 egg white

Chilled club soda

Combine gin, cream, lemon juice, lime juice, sugar, orange flower water and egg white in cocktail shaker; shake without ice 30 seconds. Add 1 cup ice to shaker; shake about 20 seconds or until cold. Strain into chilled highball or Collins glass; top with club soda.

Note: A Ramos Gin Fizz is typically not served over ice, but if you don't have a chilled glass, adding a few ice cubes will help keep the drink cold longer (although it will also dilute the drink).

TUXEDO
COCKTAIL

Makes 1 serving

1½	ounces gin
1	ounce dry vermouth
½	teaspoon maraschino-flavored liqueur
¼	teaspoon absinthe or Pernod
2	dashes orange bitters
	Maraschino cherry

Fill mixing glass or cocktail shaker with ice; add gin, vermouth, liqueur, absinthe and bitters. Stir until very cold; strain into chilled cocktail glass. Garnish with cherry.

FRENCH 75

FRENCH 75

Makes 1 serving

- 2 ounces gin
- ½ ounce lemon juice
- 1 teaspoon superfine sugar
- 2 ounces chilled champagne or sparkling wine

Fill cocktail shaker with ice; add gin, lemon juice and sugar. Shake about 15 seconds or until cold; strain into champagne flute or coupe. Top with champagne; stir gently until blended.

PIMM'S CUP

Makes 1 serving

- 2 ounces Pimm's No. 1
- Lemon-lime soda
- Cucumber strip or spear
- Lemon twist

Fill chilled highball glass with ice; pour in Pimm's. Top with lemon-lime soda; garnish with cucumber and lemon twist.

GIN SOUR

Makes 1 serving

2 ounces gin
¾ ounce lemon juice
¾ ounce simple syrup (recipe follows)
Lemon twist

Fill cocktail shaker with ice; add gin, lemon juice and simple syrup. Shake until blended; strain into chilled cocktail glass or coupe. Garnish with lemon twist.

Fitzgerald: Add 2 dashes Angostura bitters to cocktail shaker with gin; proceed as directed.

Simple Syrup: Bring 1 cup water to a boil; stir in 1 cup sugar. Reduce heat to low; stir constantly until sugar is dissolved. Cool to room temperature; store syrup in glass jar in refrigerator.

NEGRONI

NEGRONI

1 ounce gin

1 ounce Campari

1 ounce sweet or dry vermouth

Orange slice or twist

Fill cocktail shaker half full with ice; add gin, Campari and vermouth. Stir until blended; strain into chilled cocktail glass. Garnish with orange slice.

BRONX

Makes 1 serving

2 ounces gin

1 ounce orange juice

½ ounce dry vermouth

½ ounce sweet vermouth

Orange twist or slice

Fill cocktail shaker with ice; add gin, orange juice, dry vermouth and sweet vermouth. Shake until blended; strain into chilled cocktail glass. Garnish with orange twist.

SOUTH SIDE

2 ounces gin

¾ ounce lemon juice

¾ ounce simple syrup (recipe follows)

5 fresh mint leaves

Fresh mint sprig and/or lemon twist

Fill cocktail shaker with ice; add gin, lemon juice, simple syrup and mint leaves. Shake until blended; strain into ice-filled Collins glass or chilled cocktail glass. Garnish with mint sprig and/or lemon twist.

Simple Syrup: Bring 1 cup water to a boil; stir in 1 cup sugar. Reduce heat to low; stir constantly until sugar is dissolved. Cool to room temperature; store syrup in glass jar in refrigerator.

CLOVER CLUB

1½ ounces gin

¾ ounce lemon juice

½ ounce dry vermouth

2 teaspoons grenadine or raspberry syrup

1 egg white

Combine gin, lemon juice, vermouth, grenadine and egg white in cocktail shaker; shake 10 seconds without ice. Fill shaker with ice; shake about 30 seconds or until cold and frothy. Strain into chilled cocktail glass.

LIQUEURS

DON PEDRO

DON PEDRO

- 1 cup vanilla ice cream
- 2 ounces cream
- 1 ounce whiskey
- 1 ounce coffee-flavored liqueur

Combine ice cream, cream, whiskey and liqueur in blender; blend until smooth. Serve in hurricane glass.

AMARETTO STONE SOUR

Makes 1 serving

- 2 ounces amaretto
- 2 ounces sweet and sour mix
- 2 ounces orange juice
  Maraschino cherry

Fill highball glass with ice; add amaretto, sweet and sour mix and orange juice. Stir until blended; garnish with maraschino cherry.

GOLDEN DREAM

Makes 1 serving

2 ounces orange-flavored liqueur

2 ounces Galliano

2 ounces orange juice

1 ounce whipping cream

Fill cocktail shaker half full with ice; add liqueur, Galliano, orange juice and cream. Shake 30 seconds or until well blended; strain into chilled cocktail glass.

GRASSHOPPER

Makes 1 serving

2 ounces crème de menthe

2 ounces crème de cacao

2 ounces half-and-half or whipping cream

Fill cocktail shaker half full with ice; add crème de menthe, crème de cacao and half-and-half. Shake until well blended; strain into chilled cocktail glass.

GOLDEN DREAM

B-52

B-52

Makes 1 serving

½ ounce coffee-flavored liqueur

½ ounce Irish cream liqueur

½ ounce orange-flavored liqueur

Pour coffee liqueur into shot glass; top with Irish cream liqueur, then orange liqueur. (Do not stir.)

BLOOD AND SAND

Makes 1 serving

1 ounce Scotch

¾ ounce cherry-flavored liqueur

¾ ounce sweet vermouth

¾ ounce orange juice

   Maraschino cherry

Fill cocktail shaker with ice; add Scotch, liqueur, vermouth and orange juice. Shake 15 seconds or until cold; strain into chilled cocktail glass or coupe. Garnish with cherry.

SWEET RUBY

- 1 ounce ruby port
- ¾ ounce amaretto
- 2 dashes Angostura bitters

Fill mixing glass or cocktail shaker with ice; add port, amaretto and bitters. Stir 10 seconds; strain into chilled old fashioned glass half full of ice.

KAMIKAZE

Makes 1 serving

- 1 ounce vodka
- 1 ounce orange-flavored liqueur
- 1 ounce lime juice

Fill cocktail shaker half full with ice; add vodka, liqueur and lime juice. Shake until blended; strain into chilled cocktail glass or ice-filled old fashioned glass.

SWEET RUBY

MELON BALL

MELON BALL

Makes 1 serving

3 ounces orange or pineapple juice

2 ounces melon-flavored liqueur

1 ounce vodka

Frozen melon balls and fresh mint leaves

Fill cocktail shaker with ice; add orange juice, liqueur and vodka. Shake until very cold; strain into chilled cocktail glass. Garnish with melon balls and mint leaves.

AMARETTO SUNRISE

Makes 1 serving

4 ounces orange juice

1 ounce amaretto

¾ ounce grenadine

Combine orange juice and amaretto in highball or old fashioned glass; stir until blended. Add grenadine; let sink to bottom of glass. (Do not stir.)

WHITE LINEN

1½ ounces gin

1 ounce lemon juice

½ ounce elderflower liqueur

½ ounce simple syrup (page 50)

Chilled club soda

Fill cocktail shaker with ice; add gin, lemon juice, liqueur and simple syrup. Shake until blended; strain into ice-filled Collins or highball glass. Top with club soda.

MUDSLIDE

Makes 1 serving

1 ounce vodka

1 ounce coffee-flavored liqueur

1 ounce Irish cream liqueur

Fill cocktail shaker half full with ice; add vodka and liqueurs. Shake until blended; strain into chilled cocktail glass.

WHITE LINEN

LAST WORD

¾ ounce gin

¾ ounce green Chartreuse

¾ ounce maraschino-flavored liqueur

¾ ounce lime juice

Lime twist

Fill cocktail shaker with ice; add gin, Chartreuse, maraschino liqueur and lime juice. Shake until blended; strain into chilled coupe or cocktail glass. Garnish with lime twist.

VIENNESE COFFEE

Makes about 4 servings

3 cups freshly brewed strong black coffee

3 tablespoons chocolate syrup

1 teaspoon sugar

⅓ cup whipping cream

¼ cup crème de cacao or Irish cream liqueur

Whipped cream (optional)

Chocolate shavings (optional)

Combine coffee, chocolate syrup and sugar in large saucepan; bring to a simmer over medium heat. Reduce heat to low; simmer 5 minutes or until sugar is dissolved and mixture is heated through. Stir in cream and crème de cacao. Garnish with whipped cream and chocolate shavings.

RUM

BEACHCOMBER

BEACHCOMBER

2 ounces light rum

1 ounce orange-flavored liqueur

1 ounce lime juice

¼ ounce maraschino-flavored liqueur

Maraschino cherry

Fill cocktail shaker with ice; add rum, orange liqueur, lime juice and maraschino liqueur. Shake until blended; strain into chilled cocktail glass. Garnish with maraschino cherry.

DAIQUIRI

1½ ounces light rum

¾ ounce lime juice

1 teaspoon powdered sugar

Lime twist

Fill cocktail shaker half full with ice; add rum, lime juice and powdered sugar. Shake until blended; strain into chilled cocktail glass. Garnish with lime twist.

JUNGLE BIRD

Makes 1 serving

1½ ounces Jamaican or dark aged rum

1½ ounces pineapple juice

¾ ounce Campari

½ ounce lime juice

½ ounce Simple Syrup (recipe follows)

Pineapple wedge

Fill cocktail shaker with ice; add rum, pineapple juice, Campari, lime juice and simple syrup. Shake 30 seconds or until cold; strain into ice-filled old fashioned glass, tiki mug or copper mug. Garnish with pineapple wedge.

Simple Syrup: Bring 1 cup water to a boil; stir in 1 cup sugar. Reduce heat to low; stir constantly until sugar is dissolved. Cool to room temperature; store syrup in glass jar in refrigerator.

RUM SWIZZLE

Makes 1 serving

2 ounces rum

1 ounce lime juice

1 teaspoon superfine sugar

2 dashes Angostura bitters

Lime slice

Combine rum, lime juice, sugar and bitters in chilled Collins or highball glass filled with crushed ice; stir vigorously with long spoon until blended. Garnish with lime slice.

Note: Swizzles originated in the Caribbean in the early 1800s. These tall rum drinks were served over crushed ice and mixed with long twigs; the twigs were rubbed rapidly between one's hands, which was called "swizzling." Most swizzle drinks today are mixed with long bar spoons and they can contain spirits other than rum.

COCO LOCO

Makes 1 serving

4 ounces pineapple juice

2 ounces light rum

1 ounce cream of coconut

1 ounce milk

½ ounce amaretto

1 teaspoon grenadine

½ cup ice cubes

Pineapple wedge and/or maraschino cherry

Combine pineapple juice, rum, cream of coconut, milk, amaretto, grenadine and ice in blender; blend until smooth. Serve in wine glass or hollowed-out coconut. Garnish with pineapple wedge.

MOJITO

  8 fresh mint leaves, plus additional sprigs for garnish

  2 ounces lime juice

  2 teaspoons superfine sugar or powdered sugar

  3 ounces light rum

  Soda water

  2 lime slices

Combine half of mint leaves, lime juice and sugar in each of two highball glasses; mash with wooden spoon or muddler. Fill glasses with ice. Pour rum over ice; top with soda water. Garnish with lime slices and mint sprigs.

DARK AND STORMY

Makes 1 serving

4 ounces ginger beer

2 ounces dark rum

½ ounce lime juice

Lime wedge or slice

Fill old fashioned or Collins glass with ice. Add ginger beer, rum and lime juice; stir until blended. Garnish with lime.

EL PRESIDENTE

Makes 1 serving

1½ ounces white rum

¾ ounce dry vermouth

½ ounce orange-flavored liqueur

½ teaspoon grenadine

Orange twist

Fill cocktail shaker half full with ice; add rum, vermouth, liqueur and grenadine. Shake 25 seconds or until cold; strain into chilled cocktail glass. Garnish with orange twist.

DARK AND STORMY

HAVANA SPECIAL

HAVANA SPECIAL

Makes 1 serving

2 ounces pineapple juice

1½ ounces light rum

¼ ounce maraschino-flavored liqueur

Pineapple wedge

Fill cocktail shaker half full with ice; add pineapple juice, rum and liqueur. Shake until blended; strain into ice-filled wine glass or highball glass. Garnish with pineapple wedge.

CUBA LIBRE

Makes 1 serving

2 ounces rum

Chilled cola

Lime wedge

Fill chilled highball glass half full with ice. Pour rum over ice; fill with cola. Garnish with lime wedge.

GROG

2 ounces dark rum

½ ounce lemon juice

1 teaspoon packed brown sugar

2 to 3 whole cloves

¾ cup boiling water

1 cinnamon stick

Combine rum, lemon juice, brown sugar and cloves in warm mug. Pour in boiling water; stir with cinnamon stick until sugar is dissolved.

TEQUILA

CLASSIC MARGARITA

Makes 2 servings

Lime wedges

Coarse salt

Ice

4 ounces tequila

2 ounces orange-flavored liqueur

2 ounces lime or lemon juice

Additional lime wedges

1. Rub rim of 2 margarita glasses with lime wedges; dip in salt.

2. Fill cocktail shaker with ice; add tequila, liqueur and lime juice. Shake until blended; strain into prepared glasses. Garnish with lime wedges.

Frozen Margarita: Rub rim of 2 margarita glasses with lime wedges; dip in salt. Combine tequila, liqueur, lime juice and 2 cups ice in blender; blend until smooth. Pour into prepared glasses; garnish with lime wedges.

ELDORADO

ELDORADO

Makes 1 serving

2 ounces tequila

1 tablespoon honey

1½ ounces lemon juice

Lemon or orange slice

Fill cocktail shaker half full with ice; add tequila, honey and lemon juice. Shake until blended; strain into ice-filled old fashioned or Collins glass. Garnish with lemon slice.

MEXICANA

Makes 1 serving

1½ ounces tequila

1½ ounces pineapple juice

1 ounce lime or lemon juice

½ teaspoon grenadine

Fill cocktail shaker with ice; add tequila, pineapple juice, lime juice and grenadine. Shake until blended; strain into ice-filled Collins or highball glass.

MANZARITA

2 lemon quarters

⅛ teaspoon ground cinnamon

2 ounces tequila blanco

1½ ounces apple cider (nonalcoholic)

¾ ounce elderflower liqueur

Cinnamon stick

Muddle lemon quarters and cinnamon in cocktail shaker. Fill shaker half full with ice; add tequila, cider and liqueur. Shake until blended; strain into ice-filled old fashioned glass. Garnish with cinnamon stick.

ECLIPSE

Makes 1 serving

2 ounces tequila añejo

¾ ounce Aperol

¾ ounce cherry-flavored liqueur

¾ ounce lemon juice

¼ ounce mezcal

Lemon twist

Fill cocktail shaker with ice; add tequila, Aperol, liqueur, lemon juice and mezcal. Shake until blended; strain into chilled coupe or old fashioned glass. Garnish with lemon twist.

CANTARITO

Makes 1 serving

        Lime wedge

        Coarse salt

1½ ounces tequila

 ½ ounce lime juice

 ½ ounce lemon juice

 ½ ounce orange juice

        Grapefruit soda

        Lime, lemon and/or orange wedges

Rub rim of Collins glass with lime wedge; dip in salt. Fill glass with ice; add tequila, lime juice, lemon juice and orange juice. Top with grapefruit soda; stir until blended. Garnish with citrus wedges.

Note: In Mexico, Cantaritos are typically served in salt-rimmed clay pots.

BRAVE BULL

Makes 1 serving

1½ ounces tequila

1 ounce coffee-flavored liqueur

Lemon twist

Fill chilled old fashioned glass with ice; add tequila and liqueur. Stir until blended; garnish with lemon twist.

TEQUILA MATADOR

Makes 1 serving

1½ ounces tequila blanco

1 ounce pineapple juice

½ ounce lime juice

Lime or pineapple wedge

Fill cocktail shaker with ice; add tequila, pineapple juice and lime juice. Shake until blended; strain into champagne flute or ice-filled old fashioned glass. Garnish with lime wedge.

BRAVE BULL

TEQUILA SUNRISE

TEQUILA SUNRISE

Makes 1 serving

- 2 ounces tequila
- 6 ounces orange juice
- 1 tablespoon grenadine
- Lime slice

Place 4 ice cubes in highball glass. Pour tequila and orange juice over ice; do not stir. Pour in grenadine; let sink to bottom of glass. (Do not stir.) Garnish with lime slice.

MEXICOLA

Makes 1 serving

- 2 ounces tequila
- ½ ounce lime juice
- 5 ounces chilled cola
- Lime wedge

Combine tequila and lime juice in chilled ice-filled Collins glass. Top with cola; stir until blended. Garnish with lime wedge.

VODKA

COSMOPOLITAN

COSMOPOLITAN

Makes 1 serving

- 2 ounces vodka or lemon-flavored vodka
- 1 ounce orange-flavored liqueur
- 1 ounce cranberry juice
- ½ ounce lime juice
  Lime wedge

Fill cocktail shaker half full with ice; add vodka, liqueur, cranberry juice and lime juice. Shake until blended; strain into chilled cocktail glass. Garnish with lime wedge.

FRENCH MARTINI

Makes 1 serving

- 2 ounces vodka
- 2 ounces pineapple juice
- ½ ounce raspberry-flavored liqueur

Fill cocktail shaker with ice; add vodka, pineapple juice and liqueur. Shake until blended; strain into chilled cocktail glass.

CHERRY COLLINS

Makes 1 serving

2 ounces cherry-flavored vodka

¾ ounce lemon juice

¾ simple syrup (recipe follows)

Club soda

Fresh cherries

Fill highball glass with ice; add vodka, lemon juice and simple syrup. Stir until blended; top with club soda. Garnish with cherries.

Simple Syrup: Bring 1 cup water to a boil; stir in 1 cup sugar. Reduce heat to low; stir constantly until sugar is dissolved. Cool to room temperature; store syrup in glass jar in refrigerator.

BLOODY BULL

Makes 1 serving

- 3 ounces tomato juice or spicy vegetable juice
- 2 ounces vodka
- 2 ounces beef bouillon granules
- ½ ounce lemon juice
- ¼ teaspoon Worcestershire sauce
  - Dash hot pepper sauce
  - Salt and black pepper
  - Cherry tomato or lemon wedge

Fill cocktail shaker two thirds full with ice; add tomato juice, vodka, bouillon, lemon juice, Worcestershire sauce, hot pepper sauce and salt and black pepper. Shake until blended; strain into ice-filled highball glass. Garnish with cherry tomato.

MARTINI

Makes 1 serving

  2 ounces vodka or gin

  ½ ounce dry vermouth

Fill cocktail shaker half full with ice; add vodka and vermouth. Stir or shake until blended; strain into chilled cocktail glass.

Dirty Martini: Add 1 to 2 teaspoons olive brine to Martini; garnish with olive.

Gibson: Garnish Martini with cocktail onion.

SEA BREEZE

Makes 1 serving

  3 ounces cranberry juice

  2 ounces grapefruit juice

  1½ ounces vodka

    Lemon slice

Fill cocktail shaker half full with ice; add cranberry juice, grapefruit juice and vodka. Shake until blended; strain into ice-filled Collins or highball glass. Garnish with lemon slice.

MARTINI

WEST SIDE

2 ounces lemon-flavored vodka

1 ounce lemon juice

½ ounce simple syrup (recipe follows)

1 sprig fresh mint

Chilled club soda

Fill cocktail shaker with ice; add vodka, lemon juice, simple syrup and mint. Shake until blended. Top with splash of club soda; strain into chilled coupe or cocktail glass.

Simple Syrup: Bring 1 cup water to a boil; stir in 1 cup sugar. Reduce heat to low; stir constantly until sugar is dissolved. Cool to room temperature; store syrup in glass jar in refrigerator.

MADRAS

Makes 1 serving

3 ounces cranberry juice

2 ounces vodka

1½ ounces orange juice

Lime slices or wedges

Combine cranberry juice, vodka and orange juice in ice-filled highball or Collins glass; stir until blended. Garnish with lime slices.

VODKA SUNRISE

Makes 1 serving

5 ounces orange juice

1 ounce vodka

½ ounce grenadine

Orange slice

Fill highball glass half full with ice; add orange juice and vodka. Stir until blended; top with grenadine. Garnish with orange slice.

MADRAS

BLACK RUSSIAN

BLACK RUSSIAN

Makes 1 serving

2 ounces vodka

1 ounce coffee-flavored liqueur

Fill cocktail glass with ice; add vodka and liqueur; stir until blended.

White Russian: Float 1 tablespoon cream over top of Black Russian.

SALTY DOG

Makes 1 serving

6 ounces grapefruit juice

Salt

1½ ounces vodka

Moisten rim of highball glass with grapefruit juice; dip in salt. Fill glass with ice; pour vodka over ice. Stir in juice.

Greyhound: Omit salt.

MOSCOW MULE

½ lime, cut into 2 wedges

1½ ounces vodka

4 to 6 ounces chilled ginger beer

Lime slices and fresh mint sprigs

Fill copper mug or Collins glass half full with ice; squeeze lime juice over ice and drop wedges into mug. Pour vodka over ice; top with ginger beer. Garnish with lime slices and mint.

Blackberry Mule: Muddle 5 blackberries and 2 lime wedges in bottom of copper mug or Collins glass. Fill glass half full with ice; add 1½ ounces vodka and top with ginger beer. Stir until blended; garnish with additional blackberries and fresh mint sprigs.

MOSCOW MULE

BLOODY MARY

Dash Worcestershire sauce, hot pepper sauce, celery salt, salt and black pepper

3 ounces tomato juice

1½ ounces vodka

½ ounce lemon juice

Celery stalk with leaves, pickled asparagus, pickle spear, cocktail onion and/or green olive

Fill highball glass with ice; add dashes of Worcestershire sauce, hot pepper sauce, celery salt, salt and black pepper. Add tomato juice, vodka and lemon juice; stir gently until blended. Serve with desired garnishes.

WHISKEY

OLD FASHIONED

Makes 1 serving

1 sugar cube*

2 dashes Angostura bitters

1 teaspoon water

2 ounces whiskey

Lemon twist and maraschino cherry

Or substitute 2 teaspoons simple syrup (page 142). Stir simple syrup, bitters and water in glass.

Muddle sugar cube, bitters and water in old fashioned glass until sugar is dissolved. Fill glass half full with ice; stir in whiskey and lemon twist. Garnish with maraschino cherry.

HOT TODDY

Makes 2 servings

2 lemon wedges

2 teaspoons honey or sugar

8 to 10 whole cloves (optional)

1½ cups hot brewed tea or hot water

3 ounces whiskey or brandy

Cinnamon stick

Squeeze lemon wedges into 2 warmed Irish coffee glasses or mugs; stir in honey and drop lemon into glasses. Add cloves, if desired. Stir in hot tea and whiskey with cinnamon stick.

BOILERMAKER

1 ounce whiskey

1 pint beer

Pour whiskey into shot glass. Pour beer into chilled pint glass. Drink whiskey first, followed by beer.

Depth Charge: Pour 1 ounce whiskey into chilled pint glass; fill with beer.

HOT TODDY

RATTLESNAKE

Makes 1 serving

2 ounces rye whiskey

½ ounce lemon juice

¾ teaspoon powdered sugar

Dash absinthe or Pernod

1 egg white

Fill cocktail shaker half full with ice; add whiskey, lemon juice, powdered sugar, absinthe and egg white. Shake until frothy; strain into chilled coupe or cocktail glass.

HUNTER'S COCKTAIL

Makes 1 serving

- 1½ ounces rye whiskey
- ½ ounce cherry-flavored brandy
- Maraschino cherry

Fill old fashioned glass half full with ice; add whiskey and brandy. Stir until blended; garnish with maraschino cherry.

AMBER JACK

Makes 1 serving

- 2 ounces sweet and sour mix
- 1 ounce Tennessee whiskey
- ½ ounce amaretto
- Maraschino cherry

Fill cocktail shaker with ice; add sweet and sour mix, whiskey and amaretto. Shake until blended; strain into chilled cocktail glass. Garnish with maraschino cherry.

HUNTER'S COCKTAIL

IRISH COFFEE

IRISH COFFEE

Makes 1 serving

- 6 ounces freshly brewed strong black coffee
- 2 teaspoons packed brown sugar
- 2 ounces Irish whiskey
- ¼ cup whipping cream

  Whipped cream and grated chocolate (optional)

Combine coffee and brown sugar in Irish coffee glass or mug. Stir in whiskey. Pour cream over back of spoon into coffee. Garnish with whipped cream and grated chocolate.

WHISKEY SOUR

- 2 ounces whiskey

  Juice of ½ lemon
- 1 teaspoon powdered sugar

  Lemon or orange slice and maraschino cherry

Fill cocktail shaker half full with ice; add whiskey, lemon juice and powdered sugar. Shake until blended; strain into ice-filled old fashioned glass. Garnish with lemon slice and maraschino cherry.

SCOFFLAW

1½ ounces rye whiskey

1 ounce dry vermouth

¾ ounce lemon juice

¾ ounce grenadine

2 dashes orange bitters

Lemon twist

Fill cocktail shaker with ice; add whiskey, vermouth, lemon juice, grenadine and bitters. Shake until blended; strain into chilled coupe or cocktail glass. Garnish with lemon twist.

BOULEVARDIER

BOULEVARDIER

Makes 1 serving

1½ ounces bourbon

1 ounce sweet vermouth

1 ounce Campari

Orange slice or twist

Fill mixing glass or cocktail shaker half full with ice; add bourbon, vermouth and Campari. Stir 30 seconds or until cold; strain into chilled old fashioned or cocktail glass. Garnish with orange slice.

MANHATTAN

Makes 1 serving

2 ounces whiskey

1 ounce sweet vermouth

1 dash Angostura bitters

Maraschino cherry

Fill cocktail shaker half full with ice; add whiskey, vermouth and bitters. Stir until blended; strain into chilled cocktail glass or ice-filled old fashioned glass. Garnish with maraschino cherry.

WHISKEY SMASH

Makes 1 serving

    2 lemon quarters
    8 fresh mint leaves, plus additional for garnish
    ½ ounce simple syrup (recipe follows)
    2 ounces bourbon

Muddle lemon quarters, 8 mint leaves and simple syrup in cocktail shaker. Add bourbon; shake until blended. Strain into old fashioned glass filled with crushed ice; garnish with additional mint.

Simple Syrup: Bring 1 cup water to a boil; stir in 1 cup sugar. Reduce heat to low; stir constantly until sugar is dissolved. Cool to room temperature; store syrup in glass jar in refrigerator.

GODFATHER

GODFATHER

Makes 1 serving

1½ ounces Scotch

½ ounce amaretto

Orange slice or twist

Fill mixing glass or cocktail shaker half full with ice; add Scotch and amaretto. Stir about 20 seconds or until cold; strain into ice-filled old fashioned glass. Garnish with orange slice.

ROB ROY

Makes 1 serving

1½ ounces Scotch or other whiskey

¼ ounce sweet vermouth

1 dash Angostura bitters

Maraschino cherry

Fill cocktail shaker half full with ice; add Scotch, vermouth and bitters. Shake until blended; strain into chilled cocktail glass. Garnish with maraschino cherry.

WINE & CHAMPAGNE

POMEGRANATE MIMOSA

POMEGRANATE MIMOSA

Makes 8 servings

2 cups chilled pomegranate juice

1 bottle (750 ml) chilled champagne

Pomegranate seeds (optional)

Pour pomegranate juice into eight champagne flutes; top with champagne. Garnish with pomegranate seeds.

BELLINI

Makes 1 serving

3 ounces peach nectar*

4 ounces chilled champagne or dry sparkling wine

*Or peel and pit a ripe medium peach and purée in blender.

Pour peach nectar into chilled champagne flute; slowly pour in champagne. Stir gently until blended.

SHERRY COBBLER

Makes 1 serving

½ teaspoon orange-flavored liqueur

½ teaspoon simple syrup (recipe follows)

4 ounces dry sherry (amontillado or oloroso)

Orange slice

Fill old fashioned glass or large wine glass three-fourths full with crushed ice; add liqueur and simple syrup. Stir until blended. Gently stir in sherry; garnish with orange slice.

Simple Syrup: Bring 1 cup water to a boil; stir in 1 cup sugar. Reduce heat to low; stir constantly until sugar is dissolved. Cool to room temperature; store syrup in glass jar in refrigerator.

WASSAIL

Makes 12 (4-ounce) servings

¾ cup water

¾ cup granulated sugar

½ teaspoon ground ginger

¼ teaspoon ground nutmeg

1 small cinnamon stick

3 whole cloves

3 whole allspice

3 coriander seeds

3 cardamom seeds (optional)

3 cups white wine or ale

2¼ cups dry sherry

⅓ cup cognac

1. Combine water, sugar and spices in large saucepan; bring to a boil over high heat. Reduce heat to medium-low; simmer 5 minutes.

2. Stir in wine, sherry and cognac; heat just to a simmer. (Do not boil.) Strain into heatproof pitcher or punch bowl. Serve warm.

APPLE CIDER MIMOSA

Makes 1 serving

- 3 ounces chilled apple cider (nonalcoholic)
- 3 ounces chilled champagne

Pour cider into champagne flute. Slowly add champagne; stir gently until blended.

POINSETTIA

Makes 1 serving

- 2 ounces cranberry juice
- ½ ounce orange-flavored liqueur
- 4 ounces chilled Prosecco or champagne
- Orange twist

Combine cranberry juice and liqueur in chilled champagne flute; top with Prosecco. Garnish with orange twist.

APPLE CIDER MIMOSA

NELSON'S BLOOD

NELSON'S BLOOD

Makes 1 serving

5 ounces chilled champagne
1 ounce tawny or ruby Port

Pour champagne into champagne flute; top with port. Stir gently until blended.

BLUSHING BRIDE

Makes 1 serving

1 ounce peach schnapps
1 ounce grenadine
4 ounces chilled champagne

Pour schnapps and grenadine into champagne flute; top with champagne. Stir gently until blended.

MOONWALK

Makes 1 serving

1 ounce grapefruit juice

1 ounce orange-flavored liqueur

3 drops rosewater*

Chilled champagne or sparkling wine

Rosewater can be found at many liquor stores and supermarkets as well as Middle Eastern grocery stores.

Fill cocktail shaker half full with ice; add grapefruit juice, liqueur and rosewater. Shake until blended; strain into champagne flute. Top with champagne.

APEROL SPRITZ

Makes 1 serving

3 ounces Prosecco or sparkling wine

1½ ounces Aperol

Club soda or sparkling water

Orange slice

Fill wine glass or highball glass half full with ice. Add Prosecco, Aperol and splash of club soda; stir gently. Garnish with orange slice.

MOONWALK

MULLED WINE

Makes 6 to 8 servings

1	bottle (750 ml) dry red wine
1	orange, sliced
¼	cup brandy
¼	cup sugar
10	whole cloves
2	cinnamon sticks
2	whole star anise
	Additional orange slices (optional)

Combine wine, orange, brandy, sugar, cloves, cinnamon sticks and star anise in large saucepan; bring to a simmer over medium-low heat. (Do not boil.) Simmer 1 hour; strain before serving. Serve warm; garnish with orange slices.

BUCK'S FIZZ

BUCK'S FIZZ

Makes 4 servings

2 cups chilled orange juice

8 ounces (1 cup) chilled champagne

2 teaspoons grenadine or cherry-flavored liqueur (optional)

Orange slices or twists

Pour orange juice into 4 champagne flutes; top with champagne. Stir in grenadine, if desired. Garnish with orange slices.

DIPLOMAT

Makes 1 serving

1½ ounces dry vermouth

¾ ounce sweet vermouth

¼ teaspoon maraschino-flavored liqueur

1 dash orange bitters

Lemon peel

Fill old fashioned glass with ice; add dry vermouth, sweet vermouth, liqueur and bitters. Stir until blended; garnish with lemon peel.

BEER & CIDER

MICHELADA CUBANA

Makes 1 serving

1 lime wedge

Coarse salt

2 tablespoons lime juice

1 teaspoon Worcestershire sauce

1 teaspoon hot pepper sauce

½ teaspoon Maggi seasoning or soy sauce

6 ounces chilled Mexican beer

Rub rim of beer glass with lime wedge; dip in salt. Fill glass with ice; add lime juice, Worcestershire sauce, hot pepper sauce and Maggi seasoning. Top with beer.

SHANDY

Makes 1 serving

6 ounces chilled beer

6 ounces chilled carbonated lemonade, lemon-lime soda, ginger beer or ginger ale

Lemon slice

Pour beer into chilled large wine glass or pint glass; top with lemonade. Garnish with lemon slice.

BLOODY BEER

Makes 1 serving

Lime wedge (optional)

Coarse salt or celery salt (optional)

3 ounces Bloody Mary mix, tomato juice or tomato-clam juice

1 can or bottle (12 ounces) chilled lager beer

Rub rim of pint glass with lime wedge; dip in salt, if desired. Pour Bloody Mary mix into glass; top with lager.

SHANDY

SNAKE BITE

SNAKE BITE

Makes 1 serving

8 ounces ale

8 ounces hard cider

Pour ale into chilled pint glass; top with cider. (Do not stir.)

CIDER SANGRIA

Makes 4 servings

1 cup apple cider (nonalcoholic)

⅓ cup apple brandy

2 tablespoons lemon juice

1 apple, thinly sliced

1 pear, thinly sliced

1 orange, quartered and thinly sliced

1 bottle (22 ounces) chilled hard cider

Combine apple cider, apple brandy, lemon juice, apple, pear and orange in large pitcher; stir until blended. Just before serving, stir in hard cider. Serve over ice.

BLACK VELVET

Makes 1 serving

- 3 ounces chilled champagne
- 3 ounces chilled stout

Pour champagne into champagne flute; slowly top with stout.

Tip: For Collins or highball glasses, use 4 ounces of each beverage. For pint glasses, use 6 ounces of each.

STONE FENCE

Makes 1 serving

- 2 ounces dark rum, rye or applejack
- 6 ounces hard cider
- Lemon twist

Pour rum into pint or old fashioned glass; add 2 to 4 ice cubes. Top with cider; stir until blended. Garnish with lemon twist.

BLACK VELVET

THE CURE

THE CURE

Makes 1 serving

5 ounces light-colored lager

1 ounce ginger-flavored liqueur

½ ounce lemon juice

Lemon slices, fresh mint leaves and/or fresh ginger slices

Fill highball or 12-ounce glass with ice. Add lager, liqueur and lemon juice; stir until blended. Garnish with lemon slices and mint.

HALF-AND-HALF

Makes 1 serving

8 ounces ale

8 ounces porter

Pour ale into chilled pint glass. Pour porter over back of spoon on top of ale. (Do not stir.)

NON-ALCOHOLIC

GINGER-PINEAPPLE SPRITZER

Makes 4 servings

2 cups pineapple juice or cranberry juice

1 tablespoon chopped crystallized ginger

1 cup chilled club soda or sparkling water

Pineapple wedges and/or orange slices

1. Combine pineapple juice and ginger in small saucepan; bring to a simmer over medium heat. Pour into small pitcher; cover and refrigerate 8 to 24 hours.

2. Strain juice mixture; discard ginger. Gently stir club soda into juice mixture. Serve over ice; garnish with pineapple wedges and/or orange slices.

CUCUMBER PUNCH

Makes 10 servings

1   English cucumber, thinly sliced

1   cup water

½   (12-ounce) can thawed frozen limeade concentrate

1   bottle (1 liter) chilled club soda

    Lime wedges

1. Combine cucumber slices, water and limeade concentrate in punch bowl or large pitcher. Refrigerate 1 hour.

2. Add club soda and ice just before serving. Serve over ice; garnish with lime wedges.

CITRUS COOLER

Makes 8 servings

2 cups orange juice

2 cups pineapple juice

1 teaspoon lemon juice

¾ teaspoon coconut extract

¾ teaspoon vanilla

2 cups cold sparkling water

1. Combine orange juice, pineapple juice, lemon juice, coconut extract and vanilla in large pitcher; refrigerate until cold.

2. Stir in sparkling water just before serving. Serve over ice.

PINEAPPLE AGUA FRESCA

Makes 6 servings

- ⅓ cup plus ¼ cup sugar, divided
- 3 cups fresh pineapple chunks (about ½ of 1 large pineapple)
- ¼ cup lime juice
- 2 tablespoons chopped fresh mint
- 2 cups chilled club soda

  Fresh mint sprigs

1. Place ¼ cup sugar in shallow dish. Wet rims of 6 glasses with damp paper towel or rub rims of glasses with lime wedge; dip in sugar.

2. Combine pineapple, remaining ⅓ cup sugar, lime juice and chopped mint in blender; blend 30 seconds to 1 minute or until frothy. Pour into pitcher; stir in club soda. Serve immediately in prepared glasses over ice; garnish with mint sprigs.

WARM AND SPICY FRUIT PUNCH

Makes about 14 (6-ounce) servings

4 cinnamon sticks

Juice and peel of 1 orange

1 teaspoon whole allspice

½ teaspoon whole cloves

7 cups water

1 can (12 ounces) frozen cranberry-raspberry juice concentrate, thawed

1 can (6 ounces) frozen lemonade concentrate, thawed

2 cans (5½ ounces each) apricot nectar

SLOW COOKER DIRECTIONS

1. Break cinnamon sticks into pieces. Tie cinnamon sticks, orange peel, allspice and cloves in cheesecloth bag.

2. Combine orange juice, water, juice concentrates and apricot nectar in slow cooker; add spice bag. Cover; cook on LOW 5 to 6 hours. Remove and discard spice bag before serving.

METRIC CONVERSION CHART

VOLUME MEASUREMENTS (dry)

$^1/_8$ teaspoon = 0.5 mL
$^1/_4$ teaspoon = 1 mL
$^1/_2$ teaspoon = 2 mL
$^3/_4$ teaspoon = 4 mL
1 teaspoon = 5 mL
1 tablespoon = 15 mL
2 tablespoons = 30 mL
$^1/_4$ cup = 60 mL
$^1/_3$ cup = 75 mL
$^1/_2$ cup = 125 mL
$^2/_3$ cup = 150 mL
$^3/_4$ cup = 175 mL
1 cup = 250 mL
2 cups = 1 pint = 500 mL
3 cups = 750 mL
4 cups = 1 quart = 1 L

VOLUME MEASUREMENTS (fluid)

1 fluid ounce (2 tablespoons) = 30 mL
4 fluid ounces ($^1/_2$ cup) = 125 mL
8 fluid ounces (1 cup) = 250 mL
12 fluid ounces (1$^1/_2$ cups) = 375 mL
16 fluid ounces (2 cups) = 500 mL

WEIGHTS (mass)

$^1/_2$ ounce = 15 g
1 ounce = 30 g
3 ounces = 90 g
4 ounces = 120 g
8 ounces = 225 g
10 ounces = 285 g
12 ounces = 360 g
16 ounces = 1 pound = 450 g

DIMENSIONS

$^1/_{16}$ inch = 2 mm
$^1/_8$ inch = 3 mm
$^1/_4$ inch = 6 mm
$^1/_2$ inch = 1.5 cm
$^3/_4$ inch = 2 cm
1 inch = 2.5 cm

OVEN TEMPERATURES

250°F = 120°C
275°F = 140°C
300°F = 150°C
325°F = 160°C
350°F = 180°C
375°F = 190°C
400°F = 200°C
425°F = 220°C
450°F = 230°C

BAKING PAN SIZES

Utensil	Size in Inches/Quarts	Metric Volume	Size in Centimeters
Baking or	8×8×2	2 L	20×20×5
Cake Pan	9×9×2	2.5 L	23×23×5
(square or	12×8×2	3 L	30×20×5
rectangular)	13×9×2	3.5 L	33×23×5
Loaf Pan	8×4×3	1.5 L	20×10×7
	9×5×3	2 L	23×13×7
Round Layer	8×1½	1.2 L	20×4
Cake Pan	9×1½	1.5 L	23×4
Pie Plate	8×1¼	750 mL	20×3
	9×1¼	1 L	23×3
Baking Dish	1 quart	1 L	—
or Casserole	1½ quart	1.5 L	—
	2 quart	2 L	—